The Beautiful Life

Mark Anthony

Time tells us if it is love.

BURNING TREE BOOKS| Our books are lit.
www.burningtreebooks.com

Mark Anthony/Burning Tree Books

www.burningtreebooks.com

Publisher's Note: This is a work of poetry. Names, characters, places, and incidents are the product of the author's life, love, and inspiration.

Cover photo: Instagram @ilovegreeninspiration

Book Layout © 2015 BookDesignTemplates.com

The Beautiful Truth/ Mark Anthony. -- 1st ed.
ISBN 978-1544790251

For my one and only bird,
the light and love
of my life.

And you?
When will you begin
That long journey
Into yourself?

—RUMI

Contents

Part One

Part 2

Part Three

Part One

*One day love
will arrive
at your front door,
and will have
the right address*

She liked to listen to the waves
crashing into shore at sunset,
as the light slowly
fell from the sky,
and spread across the ocean
like a song.

There was something
so beautiful
in such moments,
something so gorgeously lonely
and real,
she stayed listening
to the music of the water,
long after it was dark.

The mistakes we make in love
are only the lessons we need
to discover the love that lasts;

We have to know what breaks us
before we can stay unbroken.

What you wanted from love was right,
but it was with the wrong person.

Believe me:

somebody will fall in love
with your kind of crazy.

Don't tell me again
how the world is dark and done;

Tell me instead how we
can come back from darkness,
and be reborn into the light
like a million mythical stories
the world has written,
since the day it was born.

Then tell me:

I am one of them.

She had to walk away,
not because she didn't love him,
but because she had to love herself
more.

If you are not in love,
and I mean madly
and truly in love,
with the woman
you're with,
then you're
wasting your time,
and hers,
and it's time
to move on.

Time to seek the one
who will always
take your breath
away.

She deserves the love of a lifetime
because she's a badass
with a tender heart,
and a hurricane in a teacup.

She is the kind of woman
you can count on in battle,
the kind of woman
you can get lost with
just looking at the stars.

She's the kind of woman
you read about in poems,
yet she is as real
as real can be.

If he loves you,
you won't have to wonder
why he doesn't call,
because he
will already
be there.

Million Dollar Question:

If your relationship
was a movie,
would his actions
make you want
to stay with him
forever?

Or would you
root for your character
to get over him
and move on
and find the one
who will marry her
at the end.

Hurt feelings,
if not grieved,
stay frozen inside of us
long after the loss,
until we become numb,
and end up making
the same mistakes
over and over.

But after we
face the hurt,
and let it go,
we can float
down the river
to where
we
belong.

Take a little time each day
to appreciate
the simple things in life,
and you will have
already discovered
one of the secrets
to lasting love.

Forgive yourself
for everything:

You
were only
learning
what it
means
to be
human.

Be patient with yourself,
my dear:

Sometimes it takes time
to grow into a person
who can accept
the timing of the universe,
which in retrospect
is always perfectly punctual.

Trust that one day
you will find the one
who makes
all the others
disappear.

Love is not what broke you,
it's what heals you.

It is mistaking love
for something else
that hurts.

When you meet somebody
you will know if they are sincere
if they don't play games.

Don't let anything slide.
Keep everything on the table.

If they play games,
they aren't looking for love,
and it's better for you to move on
before they play your heart
for a fool's.

You're finally at peace with yourself,
comfortable and beautiful
in your own skin,
so, please,
remain patient:

Wait for somebody who sees your light,
and honors the work you've done.

Beware of the ones
who don't know themselves,
the ones who need you
to do all the heart work for them.

There is a difference
between somebody
who loves you,
and somebody
who is afraid
to be alone.

And it means,
the world.

If he doesn't accept your past,
and inspire your future,
he shouldn't be allowed
in your presence.

All it takes
is a moment
to fall in love
with somebody
for a lifetime.

One day
somebody
will light
a match
inside you
that will
burn
forever.

Tips on Being Single:

Get a new pair of shoes.
Go for a walk without a map.
Contemplate the meaning
of the stars and moon.

Listen to the rain.
Sing a sad song.
Eat fresh peaches.

Ask yourself:

What is this
mysterious
sweetness
called life?

What is love
if it doesn't make
every inch of you
feel cherished
to the bones?

What is love
if it doesn't
begin with
yourself?

The universe
is not trying
to break you,
my dear,
it's trying
to find a way
to wake you up,
so that you
will see
what is real,
and worth
fighting for.

It takes time
to heal,
but it also
takes courage.

Sometimes
we have to slow down
and take stock
of where our hearts have been,
and ask:

"Where do I want to go next,
and who is coming with me?"

She didn't want the world,
after all,
just somebody special
to share it with.

Dear Future Self,

I hope these words find you in a better place,
where your heart is warmed by the sunlight,
and you're surrounded
by those who truly care about you.

You are the light in my life,
and even when you left,
I wanted nothing but the best for you
because that is the kind of love
you've always deserved.

P.S.

Never forget
how strong and brave you are,
and how many times
you've already saved yourself.

Sometimes,
the best way to heal yourself
is to act as if
you're more courageous
than you feel,
and in the process
discovering you are.

Once she stopped
killing herself
with whiskey,
words,
and regrets,
she started
to see
her mistakes
before they
walked
in the door.

One night,
as she walked alone
beside the river,
she heard a voice
whispering
on the wind:

*Your eyes are the color
of my dreams.*

*One day you will be,
the love of my life.*

Find the one
who answers
all the questions
in your heart
and
rest your head
softly
upon
their chest.

To this day,
I still believe
that true love only comes
when our souls
are strong enough
to receive it.

And so one day
she discovered
she was fierce,
and strong
and full of fire,
and that not even she
could hold herself back
because her passion
burned brighter
than her fears.

If you're reading this,
you're probably like me,
looking for answers to life's questions;
you want to know how
you can feel so alone one moment,
and so happy the next.

You want to know how memories
can be so beautiful and sad,
and the secret to living
in the present.

And I have an answer for you:
you just did it,
by forgetting yourself,
and just being you
imagining
these words are true;

So now, do it again
in everything you do,
until it becomes
your beautiful life.

She heard a knock on her door,
and knew that it was time.

Part Two

*And suddenly every road
led to her door,
and everywhere else
felt like nowhere.*

Then one day
no one else would do,
and my soul
went wandering
in search of you,
amid so many strangers
in the rain.

And there were
long walks alone
by the ocean,
where waves
would whisper
your name;

And when you
finally arrived
our souls met
like two rivers
that would
run together
and one day
become
the sea.

"Seduce me
with who
you really
are," she said.

"And, what began
as a conversation,
ended in love."

To build something real
with somebody
you have to be vulnerable
and open from the very start;

And if that doesn't scare
the shit out of you,
it should.

I want to tell you
that when I look at you
I feel an attraction
I can't explain.

Your body,
your mind,
your spirit,
are written
so eloquently
on my soul,
sometimes
I don't have
a need
for words,
and
I am
speechless
in your
presence.

"How do you know if it's love?"

"Maybe when you feel something
so deeply,
there are no other words
to explain it."

I love holding you
in the quiet of the afternoon
when the world slows down
long enough for us
to catch our breath,
as we listen
to the beautiful silence,
that exists between words,

when only love speaks.

Thank you for being you
in a world full
of somebody else's.

Children cry when they are hurt,
but somewhere along the way
we learn to hide our pain,
and carry our old hurts around
like stones in our shoes.

The stones keep us walking
in circles, hoping to escape
our fears,
until we face them,
grieve them,
and let them go.

Then,
once the stones are gone,
we find we can walk anywhere.

I will kiss your scars,
and make you feel
beautiful again.

Don't let anyone
make you think
you're crazy,
just because
they're frightened
that you have
the courage
to feel.

Remember that you
have always been somebody
who deserves to be loved,
not for what you do,
but for simply being
who you are.

Had you not appeared
in my life,
I don't know if I
would have ever discovered
what it means
to be completely myself.

Believe in yourself,
and stop giving your power to others
to bring you down;

The past is over,
and there is only
who you are now;

If you come from hard times,
they only made you stronger,
and that strength, my dear,
is what makes you,
so damned attractive.

The only way
to bring down
her walls
for good
is to show her
you love her enough
to climb over them.

"Aren't you afraid?"

"No."

"Why not?"

"Because having you in my life
has already been,
an irreplaceable gift."

She doesn't settle for less
than her soul deserves,
and when she sets her sights
on something,
she doesn't stop dreaming
until it's true.

And so I fell in love with her,
the same way
the universe was created,
slowly and inevitably
the way the moon pulls
the tide
closer
and
closer
to the earth
with the gravity
of its kiss.

Let me undress you,
slowly,
one button
at a time,
so that I can
hear you breathing,
and feel your quickening pulse;

Let me kiss the back
of your neck
to send a tingle
down your spine.

Let me haunt you
like the ghost
of what's to come.

Your body is a map
of my desire,
with its rolling hills,
rivers,
peaks and valleys;

Each curve
has its own legend,
and a compass,
that moves like water
in all directions,
so that your body
has taught my eyes,
my tongue,
and my fingers
that the only
destination of desire,
is in the traveling.

The most beautiful thing
about you
is your soul.

Maybe that is why
the first time
you smiled at me,
I already knew
I loved you.

Of course,
I wish that I could have saved you
from your first broken heart,
but maybe I was meant
to be the one
who helped you
pick up the pieces,
and move on.

You are more
than enough,
my dear:

You are my everything.

She came into my life like music,
and her voice
was like a familiar song
I couldn't remember,
but each time she smiled
it reminded me of another verse;

And though she won't believe me,
even on the day we met
I knew she was my favorite love song,
because her melody
was already playing on the wind,
for only my soul to hear.

Sometimes
I can't stop
thinking about you;

You are like
a delicious ghost,
haunting my body,
my mind,
and my soul.

I close my eyes
to see you,
and my skin
shivers
from the
inside out.

And I love
feeling,
this kind
of afraid.

She looks best
in the morning
wearing nothing,
but sunshine.

There is something
beautiful in the way
she makes herself vulnerable
to the world,
laughs like a child,
and throws caution
to the wind
like confetti.

But don't mistake
a wild heart as a naïve one,
or you will see
just how quickly
a clear blue sky
can turn
into a storm.

You can put on a show
for everyone, my love
with your sunglasses,
and your cool and flawless ways,
but I know what makes
your soul laugh.

I have seen your dark
and moody side
that you try so well to hide
from the rest of the world,
and I am not afraid
to kiss it.

So go ahead
and put on a show
for the world, my love,
because I know it's me
you come home to at night,
the one who loves
everything you hide
behind the curtains

My favorite people
are the ones
who let me be
as crazy as I am.

I love her,
even on bad days
when she feels
unlovable.

When you finally meet
the love of your life,
you will know
exactly why
you had
to let
the others
go.

True intimacy
is listening
so intently
to the other,
you forget
yourself.

True bliss
is falling asleep
beside the one
you dream of.

Your hand
in mine:

twin galaxies,
bound by the sun.

I feel your warmth,
and I know
that I am home.

Believe me
when I tell you
my life is nothing
without the mystery
of your presence;
your laughter,
your kisses, your caring,
and your calm,
fill me with constant wonder.

Believe me when I tell you
I knew nothing of love,
until I discovered
the magic reality of you.

She will read
your actions
like poetry,
so make sure
to always write her
poems of love.

"How did you know
I was the right one for you?"

"You were everything
I dreamed you would be,
with benefits."

"Love can be so simple
sometimes,
it is hard to believe."

I was getting
too old
to waste
my time
over
maybes.

I am yours
the way the sunlight
belongs to the sea,
the way the wind
belongs to the trees,
the way the flowers
belong to the earth.

I am yours.

I love you without knowing why,
as if for every reason I give,
there are a hundred more
that will remain hidden in mystery.

But I do know this:

You are
the only one
who had the answer
to the question
of my soul.

And so she learned
that love was something
you couldn't force:

You had to trust
that the universe
would bring your soul
exactly what it needed
to complete itself,
and only when
when it was ready
to face itself.

She's always been a free spirit,
with an unchained heart,
a cool wave,
a wild wind,
and a burning flame;

To love her
is always to embrace the unknown,
and face
the entire universe
each day
in all its mad
and love-laced
mystery.

I know I have in you,
everything a man could want,
and that somehow I dreamed you here,
but our task is not to compare
our pain or our triumphs,
but to heal ourselves,
and grow into more perfect beings,
and in so doing,
help others to heal.

By shining
the light of our journey,
we may help others
to see better in the dark.

She will never tell you
she's falling in love,
so you must learn
to read her like a book,
see the words
she writes with her eyes,
the poetry she pens
with her body.

And by the time
you've read
all that she's saying
without words,
you will have already
fallen in love.

Part Three

Love must be fierce
to be forever.

I love you
in the quiet moments
after dark,
when we hold each other
in the stillness,
listening to the sound
of forever
as it falls in rain
upon our roof.

I love you in the laughter,
and in the music,
and in all our silly conversations
coded in now and forever;

Your love, my love,
has taught me
the meaning
of the word,
forever.

I can't imagine
my life without you
anymore
than I can imagine
a life without trees, birds,
flowers or sun;

You are the wild
that grows
inside my heart.

I asked for her hand
in marriage
in a kingdom by the sea,
to walk with me
into the next chapter
of this story,
because I didn't want
to write another one
without her.

And with a tear
in her eye,
she smiled,
and she said,

"Yes."

True story

The woman I married
was waiting for somebody
like me,
as I was waiting
for somebody like her.

She had everything
I was looking for:
passion, humor, spontaneity,
kindness, and beauty;

Yet there was also
that indefinable chemistry
that exists
between two people
that pulls souls together
through all time and space;

An ancient mystery
that can't be put
into any formula,
prayer or poem,
though Lord knows,
I've tried.

I know this world
can get crazy,
lonely and sad,
but I want you to remember me as
the one who was always here for you,
even when the rest of the world wasn't.

Relationships are never perfect,
so we have to keep learning
to listen with our hearts,
and see each other's souls;

We have to be careful of ego,
pride, and overthinking:

If we can no longer listen,
or be touched by somebody's words,
it doesn't matter what we say,
because nobody feels loved.

Love is both the desire you feel
when you first meet,
as well as the patience
you will need to get through
hard times.

And sometimes love is thrilling,
and sometimes love is quiet,
and sometimes it's watching TV
alone in the dark.

And sometimes we confuse love
with the fireworks we see on TV,
and we forget the quiet side of love.

And some go on forever
searching for more thrills,
but if you want love to last,
you must honor both sides of it.

To sail into tomorrow,
you must learn to be
as patient with each other,
as the wind to the sea.

Thank you for all the reasons
I have to love you.

Thank you for your intuition,
and your humor, your passion,
and your fears.

Thank you for showing me
the beautiful truth
of your naked soul.

All of the struggles in love
are worth a single moment
of being in somebody's arms
and knowing in your bones,
this is where you belong.

There are so many beautiful you's,
I don't know which you I love more,
the you waking up in the morning
with wild dreamswept hair,
or the you leaving for work,
so polished to perfection
I envy those
who get to see you all day;

The you coming home,
so softly and tired,
as you tell me
about your day,
the you melting
like a sunset
into my arms,
as you fall
asleep.

I will never stop
being the one
who always wants
more of you.

The world always says we need more,
but the truth is we're drowning
in too much;
we don't know what's real;
we eat without tasting,
drink without quenching our thirst;

We touch each other without feeling;
We think we need just one more thing
to make us whole,
but what we really need
is to let go.
to undress, strip down,
become raw,
and hungry again for life.

We need to be so simple
a glass of water
will taste as infinite as the ocean,
and a single slice of fruit
will yield an entire kingdom of sweet.

Last night, you came to me
in a dream;

You were like a wave
sent from the sea,
donning sea foam and silk,
and singing a siren's song
the color of sky.

And your voice
made me dream of sunlight
over blue water
as I remembered
the deserted island
where we found each other,
where you found me lost
and thirsty,
and waiting
for love's saving kiss.

I am not the man I was
when we first fell in love;

I am a much better man.

I am the man
I could not have become
without you
in my life.

I love her as she is,
doing her thing;

I would never want
to control her fire;

All I need
is to be near it.

To keep a relationship
loving and alive,
you must constantly look
for the better angels inside yourself
and in the other.

You must watch your ego,
and your pride, and be
able to admit when
you're wrong,
trusting the other to forgive.

You have to learn
the difference between
a momentary lapse of childhood pain,
and the ever-present reality,
that this too, shall pass.

Your first love
is only the love
of your life,
until you meet
the love of your life.

Some say desire
always fades in time,
but I still want her body
and soul,
to kiss her skin,
and taste the saltwater
of her lips,
and the sugar
of her heart;

I can't help running my tongue
along the coastline
of her body,
and tracing the mysteries
of the earth
between
my fingers and thumb;

She is the pleasure
of a gentle breeze,
and the eye of a hurricane;
and the way she whispers
and moans
still leaves me
trembling
with all creation.

And if he loves you,
you will know it
in whispers,
and kisses,
in kind words
and caresses,
and in all
the little things
he does
to make you smile.

"How can you still love me
after all these years?"

"Because you are the one
who sees the depth of me,
and is still not afraid
to drown."

And
I love
all
the little
ways
you
make
me
feel
like
I
am
yours.

I want nothing more
than to keep traveling
this world together,
writing this love story
on our hearts
so that we can reread it
to each other
when
we're old and gray.

It doesn't matter
where we are,
my dear:
with you
it is a beautiful place.

Time is our greatest currency,
and I want nothing more
than to spend it on you.

Every morning
you are still
the first thing
I am grateful for.

There will never
be a day
I am not thankful
for the fire
you have brought
to my life,
that still warms me
to the bones,
even if I forget
to say it.

You're the most beautiful chapter
in the book of my life.

"What is so funny,
my dear?"

"You and me
and how time,
only deepens
how I feel for you."

"You mean you still
love me then?"

"Forever, and always,
my dear."

About the Author

Mark Anthony is a poet who spent the first part of his life
looking for the love of his life, and when he finally found her,
he married to her. She is the real-life inspiration
for my passion, my poetry, and my life.
But you, dear reader, are the reason
why I want to share it.

Other books by Mark Anthony:

The Beautiful Truth

Follow Mark Anthony on Instagram @markanthonypoet

For all inquires: burningtreebooks@gmail.com

Other Burning Tree authors on Instagram:

@josechaveswriting
@rubirosewriter
@eepoet
@rimbaudpoetry

Made in the USA
Middletown, DE
09 November 2017